LOVED ONES WITH DOWN SYNDROME

Lacey Hilliard and
AnneMarie McClain

Loved Ones With

Published in the United States of America by Cherry Lake Publishing Group
Ann Arbor, Michigan
www.cherrylakepublishing.com

Reading Adviser: Beth Walker Gambro, MS, Ed., Reading Consultant, Yorkville, IL
Book Designer: Jen Wahi

Note from publisher: Websites change regularly, and their future contents are outside of our control. Supervise children when
conducting any recommended online searches for extended learning opportunities.

Library of Congress Cataloging-in-Publication Data

Names: McClain, AnneMarie, author. | Hilliard, Lacey, author.
Title: Loved ones with Down syndrome / written by AnneMarie McClain and
  Lacey Hilliard.
Description: Ann Arbor, Michigan : Cherry Lake Publishing, [2023] | Series:
  Loved ones with | Audience: Grades 2-3 | Summary: "Loved Ones With Down
  Syndrome covers the basics of Down syndrome, what people with Down
  syndrome might experience, loving someone with Down syndrome, and
  showing love for others and yourself. Loved Ones With explores what it's
  like to watch loved ones go through unique and often difficult
  circumstances. Written in kid-friendly language, this social-emotional
  learning series supports readers' empathetic understanding of these
  experiences not only for their loved ones, but also for themselves.
  Guided exploration of topics in 21st Century Junior Library's signature
  style help readers to Look, Think, Ask Questions, Make Guesses, and
  Create"– Provided by publisher.
Identifiers: LCCN 2023004570 | ISBN 9781668927366 (hardcover) | ISBN
  9781668928417 (paperback) | ISBN 9781668929889 (ebook) | ISBN
  9781668931363 (pdf)
Subjects: LCSH: Down syndrome–Juvenile literature. | People with mental
  disabilities–Family relationships–Juvenile literature.
Classification: LCC RC571 .M33 2023 | DDC 616.85/8842–dc23
LC record available at https://lccn.loc.gov/2023004570

Cherry Lake Publishing would like to acknowledge the work of the Partnership for 21st Century Learning, a network of Battelle for
Kids. Please visit http://www.battelleforkids.org/networks/p21 for more information.

Printed in the United States of America
Corporate Graphics

CONTENTS

WHAT IS DOWN SYNDROME?

Your body is made up of **cells**. **Chromosomes** are in cells. They are made up of **genes**. Genes are like codes inside your body. Genes make each person unique.

Most people have 23 pairs of chromosomes (or 46 total). Someone with Down syndrome has 47 total. They have an extra copy of one of the chromosomes. This extra copy changes how someone's body and brain grow.

Down syndrome is a condition created by an extra chromosome in someone's DNA.

Down syndrome is something people are born with. Having Down syndrome is a part of someone. It is part of what makes someone who they are.

Down syndrome is something someone is born with.

Doctors aren't sure why some people have Down syndrome. It is not because of anything the parents did. Anyone can have a baby with Down syndrome.

Look!

Look at these kids with Down syndrome. They are doing something they love. People can do things in so many ways.

WHAT PEOPLE WITH DOWN SYNDROME MIGHT EXPERIENCE

Down syndrome may affect people in different ways.

Babies with Down syndrome may start walking or talking later. Some people might have a harder time speaking. Some might not speak many words or at all.

Sometimes people with Down syndrome have to work harder.

Make a Guess!

What kinds of helpers do you think are in your community supporting people with Down syndrome?

They may need to work harder to learn things. Maybe they can't always do exactly the same thing as a kid without Down syndrome. People can be different.

Kids with Down syndrome like to play and have fun. They are like all kids in this way. They play sports. They hang out with friends. They make music. They have their own interests.

Your loved one with Down syndrome may enjoy doing many of the same things you do.

11

People with Down syndrome may have health challenges. Sometimes there is trouble with their heart. There may be treatments and procedures to help.

People's lives with Down syndrome can be different. Some lives look like those of people without Down syndrome. Some of their lives look different.

Your loved one with Down syndrome may have health problems. They may be independent, or they may not. Their lives may look a lot like yours. They may look different.

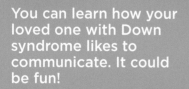

You can learn how your loved one with Down syndrome likes to communicate. It could be fun!

LOVING SOMEOME WITH DOWN SYNDROME

You can try to get to know them better. You can work to understand their likes and dislikes. You can learn how they like to **communicate**.

Having a loved one with Down syndrome can be fun. You may get to be creative. You can see new ways of looking at the world!

Think!

How could you show care to someone with Down syndrome? How could you show care to their loved ones?

15

Loving someone with Down syndrome might take **patience**. We all deserve to have people be patient with us. It can still feel hard to be patient.

Grown-ups might be busy when a loved one has Down syndrome. Grown-ups around you might not have much time. Your loved one may need a lot of attention. You might have big feelings about this. You might not get as much attention. People in the same family can need different things.

We all deserve to have people who are patient with us.
You may need to be patient, too.

You can ask for what you need. Maybe you need more time with your loved one or with your adults.

SHOWING LOVE FOR OTHERS AND YOURSELF

There are many things you can do to show love. You can show love for your loved one and for yourself.

You might find new things for you and your loved one. These can be things you both enjoy.

You might help make sure the person feels respected. You might help them feel important. This can make you feel good. You might stand up for them. You might speak up if someone says something unkind. You might speak up if they aren't getting needed support.

You might want to volunteer. You can help with Down syndrome groups. You can help at events supporting people with Down syndrome. The **Special Olympics** is one example. You can find ways to celebrate people with Down syndrome. You can find ways to celebrate them and their families.

Create!

Ask a grown-up to help you find role models with Down syndrome. What kinds of jobs do they have? Make a book with drawings or pictures of what you find.

Ask Questions!

Ask a librarian or grown-up to help you learn more. Find resources and groups that support people with Down syndrome. Can you find any of them in your community?

Things to know:

We can learn from people with Down syndrome. We can learn from their loved ones.

There are many helpers who support people with Down syndrome. Helpers support their families. Helpers can help people live in all kinds of ways.

Maybe you'll be one of the helpers one day. Maybe you already are.

GLOSSARY

cells (SEHLZ) the smallest living parts of organisms

chromosomes (KROH-muh-zohmz) found in plants and animals, contain genes that pass on traits

communicate (kuh-MYOO-nih-kayt) to share thoughts, feelings, or information

genes (JEENZ) codes inside your body that decide your traits

patience (PAY-shuhns) the ability to stay calm when you might be frustrated

Special Olympics (SPEH-shuhl oh-LIM-piks) an organization that offers training and sports events for people with disabilities

LEARN MORE

Books:

Different: A Great Thing to Be by Heather Avis; Penguin Random House

My Life with Down Syndrome by Mari Schuh; Amicus Publishing

This Is Ella by Krista Ewert; Friesen Press, Inc.

Search online for the following video resource with an adult:

Search online with an adult about the Special Olympics

INDEX

ABOUT THE AUTHORS

Lacey Hilliard is a college professor, researcher, and parent. Her work is in understanding how grown-ups talk to children about the world around them. She particularly likes hearing what kids have to say about things.

AnneMarie McClain is an educator, researcher, and parent. Her work is about how kids and families can feel good about who they are. She especially loves finding ways to help kids and families feel seen in TV and books.